THE OLD NOIS
TRUTH

The Old Noise Of Truth

JOAN DOWNAR

PETERLOO POETS

First published in 1989
by Peterloo Poets
2 Kelly Gardens, Calstock, Cornwall PL18 9SA

© 1989 by Joan Downar

ISBN 1 871471 03 6

Printed in Great Britain by
Latimer Trend & Company Ltd, Plymouth

ACKNOWLEDGEMENTS are due to the editors of the
following journals and anthologies in whose pages some of
these poems first appeared: *Iron, Poetry Matters, Poetry Review,
The Unicorn And Lions*, ed. Moira Andrew (Macmillan
Education), *Quartz, The Literary Review* and *Writing Women*.

'The Pike' was broadcast on *Poetry Now* (BBC Radio 3).

Supported by

Cornwall
County Council

For Frank Eggins,
with kind regards.
Joan Downar.
August. '89.

WITH THE ASSISTANCE OF

SOUTH WEST ARTS

For Sara & Nigel

Contents

page

POEMS FROM INDIA

10   Flying Alongside Everest
11   The Other Animals
12   At Khajuraho
13   In The Weaving Shed
14   The Music Man At Mid-way House
15   Making A Purchase
16   The Bird Sanctuary At Bharatpur
17   On The Ganges
19   Indian Gold
20   Women In Chadors
21   The Women
22   At The Women's Clinic

POEMS FROM ENGLAND

24   Outrage
25   Lost Track
26   Specific
27   In The Café
28   The Maid's Tale
29   A Proposal For Charlotte
30   An Old Lady Listens
31   Her Side Of It
32   Lilies
33   Anorexia Superba
34   Words For A Termagant
35   Her Arms
36   Women In Red Rubber Gloves
37   In 'Sixty Eight
38   Some History
39   Old Countryman
40   Farmer At Chelm
41   Lying Deep
42   Effects
43   The Hero

44 The Bear Facts
46 Byron And The Animals
47 The Pike
48 Visitation
49 Scales
50 Boys Fishing
51 The American Moon Moth
52 An Incident
53 The Glass Darkly
54 From The Bramble Hedge
55 A Capella
56 German Actors
57 The Osiris Company Performs 'Twelfth Night'
58 The Longest Day
59 Visitors
60 The Lambs
61 Double Voyage
62 Voice Of The Storm
63 Havel's Letter

POEMS FROM INDIA

Flying Alongside Everest

Flying alongside Everest, we saw
the mountains standing clear
of their gauzy ruffs, the tallest
with its tiny attendant puff
of cloud ("That's it – that's it!")
blameless on cathedral blue.

We queued up, two by two,
to snap it. The Americans'
cameras gasped. We agreed,
it was impressive. But somehow
it was like coming suddenly on faith
when you hadn't prayed nearly enough.

Tense in our shuddering machine
I thought we should have begun
in the foothills, treading
the old way on fresh snow,
but knew that spirit and flesh seldom
make such exquisite journeys so.

The Other Animals

Somewhere beyond the street cattle,
pigs, water buffalo, goats,
were the other animals:
the Indian tiger, for instance,
risen from a rug to a poundage
of dangerous muscle.

There were leaves that were not leaves
but bats, black in mid-day sun;
sly nodding stone snouts
that were nearly lions; almost snakes
reclusive and teasing.

You had glimpses occasionally:
circling kites clumped like
laboratory blood; the rank whiff
of carnivorous breath and fur
following gods in temples.

It seemed important to know
they were there, somewhere,
like whales that most of us
never see but pay to preserve,
like elephants that survived
what killed the other dinosaurs.

Carrying coins in their skin,
feeling their warmth on my back,
I knew that between the hills,
hidden in trees, Edenic creatures
never revealed to travellers lived,
indistinguishable from leaves.

At Khajuraho

In the morning we are shown sculptures,
high walls of figures, all touching
and intertwined, legs, arms, breast to breast,
to thigh, to shoulder, tongue to groin,
the guide, counting up our years, slyly
risking a joke. Some of us laugh.

The sun's erection of light beats hard
on the bodies, tenderly carved, tenderly curved
to each other, mistresses, ministrators
combing hair, applying oil, playing
with pets, their brown flesh cushioned
and sweet, engorged with pleasure.

I have to smile, regarding them, the mithuna
figures, reaching for heaven, still obedient
to Shiva's demands even after nine centuries,
and as they turn over, embracing shadow.
I could be one of them, devoted, willing,
and cast in stone, sand-dry, remembering.

In The Weaving Shed

In the weaving shed, rough and splintery,
lit with just one electric bulb,
the family is crouched on the floor,
the father, a boy of five, and one sixteen.

The twine warps rise from their fingers
to a frame at the top, the man
keeping them separate and straight,
the children running the threads across

fast and accurate: tiny pink worms
wriggling viscous tails so fine the colour
cannot be seen. Family flesh
encloses the frame, their gaze knit

to the weave. The older boy at a nod
rises and offers a sliver of wood
wound with gold and we give a rupee.
We ask to see the finished material.

They unroll from under their haunches
at the foot of the frame a stream
of ferny green with flowers, leaves,
birds and feathers in silver and gold.

I think of Hokusai's waves, of Klimt's gardens,
of Manet's pool. Hanging on the wall
are the warps of families who have died out,
their patterns never repeated or usurped.

Nothing is wasted here: a cart unloaded
in the street materialises pigs and goats;
the burned-out cars of Sikhs are stripped
to make a roof. The kites cut shapes

endlessly out of the sky; even souls
are inherited. The sinewy warps
trailing their ghosts, flick
in the amber eyes of the weavers.

The Music Man At Mid-way House

They bring us tea in stained cups;
she whispers, "Make sure it's hot
before you drink." But we drink
for politeness the tarry juice.

Bourgainvillea has been primed into trees
that explode in crimson and buttercup.
Camels travail beyond
the careful grass. Like them,

we sit nose upward, but I think
how untrue it feels. An old man
in a white turban asks
if we like Indian songs. No-one replies,

but he sings anyway, a long thread
from further back than we can boast,
the one string closing my throat.
I look for change, and find none.

His involuntary gift is what I've seen
reaching towards me in streets and palaces,
touched, smelt and drunk
with the abandonment of trust.

Leaving the empty cups, we trail
back to the coach. What meeting was there?
A few notes shared with a man
who made my eyes water the dust.

Making A Purchase

She wanted to buy beans,
I wanted tea. Brought
to the small open-fronted shop,
we sat waiting while the proprietor
served his queue. Brown eyes
wondered at two white women
far from the market and the big streets,
threading glances and tongue tied.
(He was slender, in a white dhoti.)

On the shelves we saw tins
of Oxo, packets of Lux,
matches, Camp coffee – old names
from an Empire childhood,
stained, crushed and rimed in dust.
We named them affectionately,
softly, so as not to insult,
and at last he came to serve us.
(He was shop-keeper polite.)

He shovelled beans, found the tea,
bearing that year's date,
Lion Brand from Lipton's, wrote
down the prices, added tax, and we paid,
mute, without the formality of smiles.
Such tenuous contact done, we trailed
along streets dank with piss and shit
clutching our thin nourishment.
(I would not know his face again.)

The Bird Sanctuary At Bharatpur

The rider agreed to take two fat white women
in a rickshaw, standing his six stone on the pedals.

Properly called Keoladoe Ghana, it unrolled
its dry grass and scummy lakes, its golden acacia –

an effortless cliché. He paused often
to point to invisible birds, to take pictures

of white spots. It says here, she murmurs,
that during winter birds come from as far as Siberia.

He sweats; the sky is white like wadding;
we travel gorged with heat, trailing

a peculiar muffling dust. And there,
a glimpse of spoonbill, pochard ducks,

a pied kingfisher, snake-necks, vultures,
bats hanging like rotting leaves, scarlet

minahs and a veil of cranes, grey and white
shivering above the trees. A tally board

counts the millions of feathers blasted by
emperors, governors and ambassadors. These

brilliances entertain black infinity,
make, under the kite's eye, Indian palaces.

On The Ganges

Stepping over
flesh and bone
strange as mastodon,
the human voice's
upward cadence
starting antiphonal
guilt, the nicely
composed pictures
breaking in panicky
flakes, board the shallow
boat that gives easily
on the oily water.
A priest's orange dress
colours the ghat; some women
wash themselves and then
their clothes. A man coughs
and cleans his teeth
with a brown twig.
Like rolled-up carpet
a bound corpse waits
on the steps; white mourners
sit round burning wood;
a dead foot twitches
and turns on its spit.
Marigolds with candles
float from a mercenary
child. The stone lingam
with its ejaculated grass
is watered idly by a woman
passing, and cow pats
identified by palm-prints
dry in the sun that turns
from blood to bronze.
The oarsmen paid,
the forged flesh
has to be passed.
An anxious woman wears

an emerald sari,
living in a jewel.
The holy river bears
its manifest of filth.
And I find myself recomposing,
stepping over.

Indian Gold

The golden oblong pouches of the bean tree,
seeds outlined like coins in silk,
fade to rags as the sun falls,
and the sky, dust-laden, reddens
to sore skin.

In the soft sandalwood scented hotel room
I listen to jackals baying, to the cry
of withered children, to beggars' curses,
the riches of India folded
in decent darkness.

Women In Chadors

It was as if the cobbles boiled black,
the women in their chadors marching
down the street protesting solidarity with what
kept them veiled. No good laughing
at what seemed a pathetic lack
of self interest when we are all guilty of
tying ourselves up religiously in that
voluminous uniform we call love.

The Women

The women wrap their legs in soft
dark cotton. If you look closer you can see
the odd stripe, the tiny unaggressive
pattern, a diamond, a blown flame.

Their breasts have disappeared in folds
of black, of brown, or iron red. They are coming
down to earth. They are putting off
extremities and appendages, they are homing

in on themselves. The hours belong to them,
undemanding. They begin to know their power,
to unravel it. Words spin. They make soft
wool, fine silk, fibres true to their source,

and eventually they put them on, brilliant
as goddesses, and walk in the light in the fields
so others will know them. Shy and cumbrous
as bullocks, gods move away from their path.

At The Women's Clinic

We come singly, in twos, threes,
past the flying powder
of concrete-mixers (there always seems

to be some kind of mending
going on here) and the men
look up slyly under white lashes, vetting

our legs. We enter a shrine
with flowers, calm,
are given instruction, uttering in private

the most powerful, sacred
words, worshipping
the snake embracing its staff. And will leave,

colluding in jests about fannies and paps.
I think of the card
with erotic carvings, a love note on the back,

sent home from India that disappeared,
fingered, perhaps, and mangled
by men who swear by what they fear.

POEMS FROM ENGLAND

Outrage

A woman, legs akimbo, lies
on the turf, dying back to it.
Scavenging sheep have ignored her, but not
the birds or rats or beetles. A nosy walker
smells her last scent.

All her gifts have been forcibly
taken, passion, tenderness, these more
precious than the blue necklace, jellied breast
or blackening flaps of the private
wound can ever have given or meant.

And love has failed her, not her own,
but lack of it in her assailant. That,
and language peeled away from
thought and feeling, words that like monsters
became noisy and innocent.

Lost Track

Trains articulate quietly between the banks
then stop with exhausted sighs.
Clouds of may, branches of vapour
mingle their breath.
    In the clicking silence
she hears grasshoppers, a single lark,
the imitative cuckoos of pigeons, sees
the blurred passage of wasps in their
fin-de-siècle corsetry.
    Juices squeeze
in the sun's suspension, from her skin,
from the orifices soon to be breached
by the man hiding behind the trees
who will blame the time he lives in.

Specific

"There is no such thing as 'crime', only crimes." Louis Blom-Cooper, QC in the 3rd Tanner Lecture on 'The Penalty of Imprisonment', quoted in *The Guardian*, 11.12.87.

Comforting to think the murderer is pure
even when fingering the knife
until the blood actually runs;
and the gun's
instant accolade on a full life
ignores what the family's had to endure.

Applied to love, it makes nonsense of saints, the main
of romance, charity's poor
earnest attempts; is dully amnesic,
needs a specific
demonstration, a spoken cure,
to her, to him, again and again.

In The Café

Having the proprietor's welcome, they came in,
ushered to little tables for tea and cakes.
The helpers ordered. Lily made her choice
despite them – chocolate gateau. Jean
and Betty fondled the salt. Gladys
cradled her rocking buttocks. Warned
to be quiet, they hissed questions, snorted,
gulped and belched. The other customers
invented conversations. The women, with spoiled
faces like flesh pulled on too carelessly,
filled the room with sounds of appetite;
their clumsy hands from unreflective clothes
hung tenderly with generous caresses over
the clean perfection of the café cat.

The Maid's Tale

Jane's testimony proves the folk-lore
accurate: the gentleman with the gravid wife
really did try the bath and bedroom door.
Would the maid surrender? She would not.

Later, burdened with house and child,
Jane left them in the lurch, traditionally the poor's
only revenge: to run to their own wild
withholding the body, the rich man comfortless.

Burrowed in her bungalow, over-hot,
Jane chuckles now – *The dirty dog*! A sense
of her ninety years enriches the air, defined
the more sharply by her coming absence.

A Proposal For Charlotte

When the small sharp chin was softening
to repeat itself, his question came.
Her head lifted; it was an achievement
of sorts. A skittering re-adjustment of home
took place, and she assented.

Of course the monthly mess was rarer,
the sheets became wider, their spaces
more demanding, but still the re-written life
had a child as climax, or nearly, and her death
was never what he'd intended.

An Old Lady Listens

(The oldest man in the world interviewed by a pretty young
woman, sang to her: "I should like to take you into my bed.
If you want a baby, you know what to do.")

Half moons of water slop
in the light, her rings shine.
Animals and children troop
at a distance; time

is nearing with its tackle.
She lies in her cool bed
thinking how little
she could echo his song; she'd

finished with lust, its blain
and bluster, with no regret.
She could be hooked by pain
from other causes, but what

was left of that great thrash?
No gorgeous crescents gleam
in porcelain, but plain fish
patrolling a long ocean.

Her Side Of It

After the first separation
I stood upright and walked
in colour and light so pure
I knew this was its very
first human inspection.

I put things in their place,
made them memorable with names:
rose, green, violet,
gold, earth, sky.
They escaped sometimes.

I measured distances, yearned
for closeness. Creation burned
with helpless numb
brilliance, seeking release,
a valediction which I shared.

But you followed, wanting
to know what I saw and heard,
what I whispered, jealous
of the bird on my hand, even
of the poor well-meaning worm.

Scents and sense intermingled –
oh, the joy of making opposites
contiguous! You knew there was more
than you had discovered, so I gave
you my gift, and you wept.

Pressing against your side
I staunched the still tender
wound, and the green apple, slightly
bitten, bobbed ambiguously
in your breast, like a heart.

Lilies

There are no lilies in the garden:
lilies are grown abroad. She is surprised
less by the visitor than by his burden.

Those cool trumpets, like music claiming
her ears, draw her in, impaled
on the musky scented ring

of yellow filaments, a coronet that covers
her face with gold, a living icon.
Blood will stop, then. Other

women are making hasty ceremony
of meals, making a ritual of work.
She sits in unaccustomed lethargy.

It is awesome, what she has undertaken.
Somewhere a woman steps among narcissi
on the way to darkness, shaken

by the betrayal of a man's turned head;
a village Mary's buried under a tumulus
of flowers. These must be discounted.

She looks at the lilies that were left,
unseasonal, unexpected, touches
the hopeful trembling stamens of her gift,

and finds herself with song.

Anorexia Superba

Careful how you tread, some of my best blooms
are on the floor. I keep them low
to start with, let them see the light
gradually. I can't stand that leafage
too fleshy. Oh yes, some fail to flourish;
you'll see them on the compost. They'll be
of use in a humble way. The wife
takes a few, decorates her window sill,
can't bear to think her seed lacks goodness,
lacks "virtue" to use the old word, cries
when they turn yellow and droop. I wait
until she's out, hustle them off, but
"Where's my Rose?" she calls, "Where's Iris?"
I don't answer. Here's where you'll find me,
admiring this slender stem, these white hands,
this light-filled face. I stoop to kiss it.
How can I resist? My creature, my creation.
And the tender essential plant? Selective
feeding is the thing; it takes what it wants.
You ask about purity. Guaranteed.
When it flowers I pinch the ovaries,
discourage stamens. Ah, we're alone.
Oh blossom, stay for me, stay for me!

Words For A Termagant

The better artists keep it in,
the stripped eye, the stretched lip;
that little French fellow in the Follies
saw it under white spotlights which blinded
the fuddled punters to its anger.

You see it on the bus; you don't often
hear it – the cantrip, the witchy words,
the desperate huff, the quick warm
subliminal howl. Come, let fly.
Raise your voice, let it clear the roofs,

the aerials. Sweep the sweet black sky
with your histories of grief, your hollow
loves, betrayals. Tinder the grim north blore
before you return to your sinistrous shell,
naked, uncompromising scold.

Her Arms

She'd never have seen them, but her arms
were like those painted by artists,
Spencer, Burra, Vanessa Bell,
Women of weighty flesh, forms

that generously filled a space.
They floated sheets on to a line,
whitely vaporous from a squawking mangle,
catching the currents. Her waist

inched outwards. If she looked
up behind her she saw creamy
cliffs of chalk and if to her apron,
the sea's white glare as it sucked

on light. I do not know if she meant
one day to leave – her strength, like the painted
women's could have fleshed out
canvas – but perhaps consoled with a faint

reflection of freedom she took a chance
on a life of chores, just noting
swallows pegged to telephone wires
when clouds were the image of innocence.

Woman In Red Rubber Gloves

"Archaeologists have discovered aboriginal rock paintings in
a limestone cave system in Tasmania which they believe to be
among the world's oldest. The team believes the art work, a
series of 15 red ochre outlines of the human hand might be
more than 14,000 years old." – News item from *The Times*

Quintessential tool, to hold,
to grasp, to pick, pluck,
to sniff out fur, rock,
to spring blood and water;
to beat, block, to warn,
welcome. When you took
red clay, cut it away
on the cave wall, it became
thought; it became not
you, it could be blamed,
praised, spoken and named.
But – fifteen times!
Ecstasy, this power.
And I, needing to write,
put down the pen, excuse
myself with picking, holding,
beating, folding; dam up
blood and water, warn
and welcome. Caught red-handed.

In 'Sixty Eight

In 'sixty eight I was gorged on chateaux,
sunny fantastics, long bleached of serious blood,
and found myself wooed beside Loire's flood,
that placid, shallow possession of sand, less
river than lake. Saucisse, truite mousse,
tempted my lips, whilst his prepared articulate
advances. Driven in a car as stripped and springless
as a tumbril, I listened, only half understood
the message, but I knew that on this occasion
I would not lose my head, there would be no
surrender. And by May I was home, while the sets
were torn up for barricades in Paris streets.
So I missed the feast of freedom, and the passion.

Some History

We might have lived by the sea:
each day she rose like a tide
fierce and predictable, cleaning, sewing,
and went out burdened, nodding and exhausted.

We walked carefully on the beach
but the cliff didn't fall, there was no
quick-sand, just the tide to be watched
and in between, the fathomless meeting

of water air cloud their sameness
their possibilities the occasional gem
star anenome before the rush
of sussurous anxiety – cash, cash.

"Do something useful that'll earn you money",
she'd say, before we buried her laughing,
just as we'd buried our poems, our dreams,
agreeing: natural laws are cousins

to reason. She came inland last night
in a dazzling skirt of spray to needle
a bottle of ink that I clutched in a fist
as tightly coiled as an ammonite.

Old Countryman

He stands on the lane he knew
as Dumbledyke which now nameless
returns fields to the metal highway
where the mouth of the quarry was.

Closer to earth than the labourer
on the farm, he blew the mineral
from its bed and powdered it
in the grinding stones, precise as grain.

Bits of it still lie in fields, edge
garden beds, white rods enclosing
brilliants, grey masses netted
with rust like some unrecognisable

animal offal. He picks some up,
his simple narrative silenced
by the traffic and the pylon, clamped
across the fallen mouth of the quarry.

Farmer At Chelm

March, and the nearby copse
is stripped so thin I can see
it clear from edge to edge.
Harsh hiding place, it stops
the heart's clip, but not so fearfully
as these hearth bricks, blood-red,
smeared with a smoke that's dredged
from the earth, a sickening flood said
to be human sacrifice. I don't know.
Does gopher wood preserve the cries
over and over of those who survived the rise
of biblical water? Does fire still burn
the dead in our farm walls? Daunted,
I plan the harvest, a nice hope, sow
reconciliation long after, turn
my head from the charnel pall. Am haunted.

Note: A Nazi extermination camp at Chelm in Poland was completely obliterated during the war, its stones used to build a farmhouse and its ground planted with trees.

Lying Deep

After the theft, the victim's eyes let flow
tight oceanic tears, and I was left
with two suspects. One I let go,
a slow child – out of the room, too,
at the crucial time. The other I'd harrow
until he dropped the watch. Delicate, bijou,
with aquamarine eyes and gold cropped
hair, he knew I knew his guilt – an expertise
much practised – but my questions stopped,
drowned in the blank blue of those eyes an analyst
would have found quite pure, while the sound
of No and No curved the classroom walls. I missed
the old noise of truth, which now unnerved
even the believing, and wondered when somewhere in the boy's
depth, a coelacanth would splash in surprised birth.

Effects

Eight months after the thread tailed off
and snapped, we three women sit
round the boxes, dipping as into yolk
or water, bringing up heavy cloth.

Three piles of papers on the fender,
the sofa and sideboard: letters,
notices, poems, the accretions loom,
yellowing on a singular tangled life.

Busy, intent only on this rough
unweaving, we glimpse nonetheless
unexpected, unaccented words of praise,
a former beauty, smiles, promises.

And more: the finicky obsessive notes
of loathing – even latterly, even ourselves,
hospital visitors, bringing grapes and flowers,
hated for seeing that fleshy unravelling.

Our letters surface, too bland it seems
now, to appease the rage that meshed
the last poems so harshly. Drained,
we sip tea, meditate on the three piles.

We want to make something of this, something
new and worthy, egg-smooth, achieved,
but the final poems tear the fabric apart,
and her colours are evasive and already changing.

The Hero

He loved parties, any gathering that folded him
into its noise and laughter, one of the lads and lasses,

allowing him to forget the awful mess-up that was Jim,
happily reviling Tory criminals and asses.

He loved the Party, too; the Red Flag would brim
his eyes, the thought of all those toiling masses.

He counselled a little himself, spun history in his own
vein to wondering children until forced

into the hospital, a long sleep. His women had grown
to be mothers, were patient, kind. His worst

crime was fecklessness, but this and more they'd known
listening to the flood of Celtic babble that burst

from his lips: language was music, was movement, postponing
a deeply desired oblivion. The Party, tried

by excesses, discreetly retired him. Ironically he'd sing,
"It's no go, my honey lamb", and he died,

having reached fifty when neither love, faith nor reason
could help him, in his bath, in a red tide.

The Bear Facts

We have returned, you see, minus
our friend. Allow us a while
to breathe: this air is warm and scented with fat and vinous
welcome. There, every storm over every Arctic mile
invaded the lungs with pure
ice. This he could endure,

loving plain, elegant, classic
beauty. We often smiled
seeing him pale and transfixed at the glimmering waste,
    thoracic
comfort abandoned, Styx'd almost. The Polar wild
enchanted him like a fairy-
tale. We watched him, wary,

and not quite confident, although
he performed his duties and took
excellent pictures of skua, cormorant, shag, of snow
in purple shadow, the newer drifts of it. He forsook
the tent to capture hares
on film. But his passion was bears,

the great creamy long-nosed
Ursus Polaris, small-
headed, prehistoric-bodied. Modestly he supposed
our knowledge. His was folkloric. Increasingly, all
his talk was of them: giants
of the animal world; science

had no discovery so
magnificent. And then,
one beast, a male, sweet as an Eskimo,
began to haunt us for stale food. We'd count ten
as he photographed and shout
him in. But he'd go out

again and again to gaze
at it, its beauty calling
him. Until it turned and struck and his face was a maze
of blood. Shouting, we churned through the snow to the
   mauling
but he begged us not to kill it:
"Too beautiful to die." To will it,

your own death, like that
takes courage, and to revere
creation absolutely is rare. Our collective hat
goes off to him. Astutely we've recovered his film. Here,
bring us some wine. And I am
hungry for the roast lamb.

Byron And The Animals

The man loved animals – that much was certain.
They lived, you might say, firmly cheek by jowl.
You'd come upon them roosting in a curtain,
a parrot, parrakeet, some brilliant fowl
exotic, rich as the Afghan costume girt on
its owner, causing many a serving man to howl
at the droppings, wishing he could nobble 'em –
but in those days there wasn't a servant problem.

Then there were peacocks, guinea hens, macaws,
an Egyptian crane that must have taken headroom;
a crow, an eagle, falcon, – one must pause
to wonder which would share his bedroom
when ladies came to stay: would he perforce
ruffle their feathers in the said room,
egg them to ecstasy or call them chicken,
even as candle smoke the air'd thicken?

And visitors would have to brave a staircase
that monkeys, foxes, mastiffs called their territory.
Small wonder the occasional bare-faced
signore made retreat, his fast trajectory
overseen by Tita's mighty hair-based
visage, sharing the creatures' natural history.
And Byron once, like any Sherwood Forester,
loved a bear as much as a Cambridge chorister.

Tenderly he would care for this menagerie
as if their simple presence formed a mask it
consoled him to assume – (the little badger he
kept on a chain, three geese in a hanging basket
behind the carriage moving to Genoa). Savagery
he kept for men and women – it was a task he
relished, but these idiosyncracies of our creation
he respected with entirely human passion.

The Pike

The field unrolled an animal stink of cows.
A grid of gossamer crossed it, flashing
Morse in a code I couldn't untangle,
and the river was only just white.

I saw the fish in the sewing of straw-work
on the bank, glistening plastic and glass –
I thought dead – but its long snout
quivered and the liver-red of gills

peeped. The silver jacquard knit
with pale lemon suns was snagged
with twigs, its eye mud. Could it
have jumped, this foot-long jack,

from its element? Could some god-playing
angler thinking to save his sport
have left it on the bank? Another god,
myself, slipped it carefully back.

And I thought – a lover's traces on my hand –
how the pike's victims might justly question
their theology, as I do, having friends snapped up
in a pattern none of us can understand.

Visitation

Coming into the room I see,
housewifely, spots of mucus,
slate blue and cream, seed
husks screwed up and squeezed
from a tiny anus, only it takes
a moment before I look for the bird.
The windows are wide, a big
wind scours across the bed,
the desk, the chest. I look
for a handful of hot feathers,
a cold spread fan, and find none.

Tales tell of migrant birds
trapped in houses beating their wings
to rags in fright until caught
by cool-blooded pale gods
and put to flight. No triumph here.
The room has seen accident put right
by avian intelligence, my absence.
So briefly host, I collect, excited,
the evidence of passage.

Scales

The propagating frame, warm
through winter, showed its red
eye every day.
The visitor discreetly fed
on the frail plants, came
through the portal it had made
in half an inch of wood and stayed
unseen. Catalogues of seeds
made sitting-room parterres; we saw
ivory petals, peach,
rose and azure as hoar
furred the branches, beads
of ice became the broad
garden frame, and put abhorred
poison down. In time the rat
emerged, golden brown
with heaving flanks in agony
to die. (But have you known,
they said, the cornered rat,
lip-curled, caught in corn,
the shuddering image, born
of ancient contracts, with your throat
its target?) Beautiful and dead,
belled with poison, plucked
clean of fear its head,
its pale hands; its route
blocked up: the seeds we spread
will riot in gold and blood red.

Boys Fishing

Right at the pier's end the boys fish.
The North Sea is nearly idle,
the sun a mineral glow.

They stand or crouch perilously low,
or so it seems, casting, casting
impatient lines, their bait

parcels of ruby flesh cut
from a mackerel, and they ignore
whoever watches them –

the crowds escaped from rented rooms,
the fantasists, the exhausted, those
who need salt in their lives. They

keep their eyes on the sea, play
their lines with ferocious care, a metaphor
for all they desire, and know

they cannot have, and will not, no,
not ever. Gulls scratch the glassy sky.
A dab is caught.

Silently – nothing to do with sport –
a boy tears out the hook and stamps
on its roundness with his boot,

Briefly the sun warms on its route
downward the faces of boys and men,
charging them with light.

The American Moon Moth

We walk in his garden towards a shed,
our feet tangling borage and nettle.
Here are stick insects, terrapins,
worms and lepidoptera.

A last American Moon Moth, creamy
cone of fur between its powdery jade-
milk wings lies dead. He tells of love
long-nurtured and betrayed, makes

of his pain a gift. Wood's healing saps ooze,
clam under hot sun; all creatures sleep but
one. I ask him why he keeps it,
and he shrugs: its beauty, adds,

being fed as a chrysalis for life
it never eats, just breeds and dies. We walk
in sudden cool past buddleia,
summoning the errant son.

An Incident

Armed with a gun, looking for pheasants
he enters the garden, a brace
of days in hand for sport. There is frost;
the clouds are brilliantly edged,
the air condenses to deep blue as if space
were compressed. There are hooks, gaffs,
blades, hounds. I hardly breathe,
feet among sharp leaves, as if to accost
him might offer the birds, as if I, wedged
under branches, might offer him death.
At last departing, he snorts, spits, laughs.
The air becomes milky, the land a pleasaunce.

The Glass Darkly

The glass darkly
shows the bird a new mate.
He attempts to free her, fly her

through the glossy
surface, through reflection, through an
intelligence that does not sing.

Attack. Attack.
The bright beak's mad persistence
dreams its dictionary's dumb

cantatas will
break into ousel music,
to eggs hatched in a saint's warm hand.

Note: An Irish legend recounts how St Kevin was praying when a blackbird laid her eggs in his outstretched hand, and he knelt without moving until the eggs were hatched and the birds flown.

From The Bramble Hedge

It is two o' clock. The pin-head spider
is sure his life is long, as long
as his six legs. The fly,
feeding on blackberries is convinced
he is meeting God, eye to eye.

A Capella

After the Magnificat,
the child murmurs,
    holds his breath, sobs.
The little chestnut cat,
(its double is at home)
    sycamore sheep, walut camel, drop,

their consolation gone.
She rocks him on her lap.
    Nunc Dimittis fails:
ears prick for the lone
cry raising mishap,
    ennui, grief, all else

that has to be contained,
counterpoint to the hymn
    they're singing now. Yes,
like a sermon he entertains,
brings it all home,
    humble and fatherless.

Rosy-faced she pulls
his jumble-sale vest
    decently down. He sings a new note.
Outside, the sheep leave wool
on the hawthorns, enough to invest
    him in Saville Row suits.

German Actors

The young actors give their play,
a play-within-play: jeans and leather
change to short black trousers, armbands
with red swastikas (the scruff of my neck
rises like a dog's). The fascist one
is still sniffing out his prey; now
it's a Turk, then a Jew. The harsh
language that primed English
throats once crackles on the ear,
a continental imperative; our sweet Celt
blurs the issue, makes doubt possible,
alternatives, deferred conclusions.

I remember a thin Lithuanian
Jewish boy who appeared at school
with the evacuees. His voice excited us,
its new vowels, our own words
made strange. And when he quickly
died, no-one ever told us why –
The War, that vague and self-sufficient
thing we lived with, got the blame.

Now, I see these youths bravely
donning swastikas. The gentle little Jew
who never became a man sits
among them, deflecting absolutes.

The Osiris Company Performs 'Twelfth Night'

That summer clowned perversely: here
a green and peaceful garden, a girl
growing in love; there war
and distantly bereft and anxious parents.

Sweet chestnuts lined the walk, their pinkly
flowering parts offering unrationed
honey, and conflicts near the heart
went on testing extremities, slipping

on roles only that age would allow,
living on each day's bright
edge, hogging the natural mirror.
Against the rose-pink brick the company,

six women and some dogs, prepared
their play, doubling and re-doubling
male and female, so it should have been
confusing, but at the end we sighed, seeing

so many harmonies and aware too
of a residue, something we could not name,
a what-you-will, something that properly
belonged to spring and autumn, that sat

awkwardly centre stage in blazing
sun, muffled in velvet and ruff,
and would have seemed just as false – their lap
dogs wore brocade – in falling winter rain.

The Longest Day (for G. C.)

On this midsummer day, with the most light,
the most green, you say,
"One will not be remembered –"

I without child, yours without issue,
and both sensibly reconciled
to the stoppage of blood.

My tongue halts; I want to speak
of the perpetual waltz
of atoms – there

in the photographs which trace your likenesses,
the innumerable family drafts
that make your face,

and how a larger dance will orchestrate
another familiar circumstance,
a recognition:

I think I know you. Already the years
have trailed us, let us go
like made music

to sing one day in this mind
or another; and made things –
furniture, silver,

will keep the press of our hands, the sweat
of love, the stress
of usage.

We validate our immortality
ourselves, we cannot wait
for it. And here's

our most light, our most green,
incomparably true and bright
midsummer's day.

Visitors

We close the door on the doctor
and his companion the specialist
who are professionally pessimistic.

Our clock is silent; it moves
slyly but at this moment
appears to have stopped. The tick

if it could be heard is of two
hearts tapping a message
of resistance. The house

is empty of all but ourselves
drenched in a worn sun.
My breathing quickens with his.

Our protest, our disbelief
is the quiet routine of food,
conversation and sleep.

Night brings relief but
at once he stirs, trembles,
his words forced out, afraid,

"Who are you – who?" as if
he answered a knock, as if
he guessed a name. Be

well, my love, I pray. Day
comes, laying its still, pale
light on us like a scar.

The Lambs

In the dark shed, partitioned off
in three compartments are the lambs:
the runts, the orphaned, those who cannot suck.

Biblical Jacobs whose wool is soft,
Tetzels bristling under the hand,
opening the Spring with their cries. Sated, they lick

the hand that will kill them tenderly to eat
their unpolluted flesh. On trees outside
doves mimic the angel's visit, brood on lilies;

the air is pungent with the sweet
eastern scent of poplar, and you breathe
through blood and water that the doctors ease

from your side. This Easter I shall sing
of resurrection in this small
English place, resenting the old idea

of sacrifice, feeding you, marvelling
at your persistent flesh refusing to fall
to being here – and agonisingly, not here.

Double Voyage

The bed is changing, this Spring, from pleasure-craft
to hulk, anchored, vulnerable and listless.
Its busy rituals over, it concentrates its lift
and fall, lift and fall with a purity of purpose
that allows no illusion of voyage.

Yet decked in white, you patrol each day
weathering the encroachment of implacable storms
and must, surely, see a horizon play
its doubtful light. Comfort is not in my arms;
alone, you are finding the mariner's courage.

And I, not you, through a porthole in a dream
see a bird hovering, intent, something between hawk and owl
with eyes that spur my immobility, seemed sent
to start me journeying, with a yawl
of silent agony and rage.

Voice Of The Storm

When the wind rises the floors crack,
the house adjusts itself,
gives a millimetre of brick,
leans on its lost cellars.

Inside is like being in a large ear
puzzling out the diction
from a huge mouth of air
that carries promising language.

Outside, clouds roll with apocalyptic
speed; ancient beeches
tremble. I expect to speak
some fierce angel,

unsheathed, with an exceptionally pure
and understood message.
But the syllables of storm are
muffled, untranslatable,

and the angelic voice, if there is one, is tame
and domestic. The furore
over, the house is the same
hushed ear, listening.

Havel's Letter

He said, apparently, I must eat less,
exercise more, study the Bible, read Shakespeare.
He was in prison.

I place small violet cubes in neat tin lids
on the floor of the outhouse and shut the door.
He wrote the words to his wife like a promise
but they were for himself to hear.

Indoors I prepare small mouthfuls for a sick husband
and then walk on the hill.
The sun is prolific, and even the fungi
blossom rose-pink, rat-brown,
and the thorns flare wickedly up like a witch's hair.
Birds release song in a chain running
across the country. I haul myself up
along it and back to my twin tasks,
to the prisoner's familiar words.